ENDANGERED SPECIES

Text by Sarah Lovett

John Muir Publications
Santa Fe, New Mexico

Special Thanks to
Wm. Robert Irvin, Counsel, Fisheries and Wildlife Division, National Wildlife Federation
Tom Smylie, Assistant Regional Director-Public Affairs, U.S. Fish and Wildlife Service
Dale Belcher, Curator of Herpetology, Rio Grande Zoo
William L. Gannon, Collections Manager, Museum of Southwestern Biology, University of New Mexico

John Muir Publications, P.O. Box 613, Santa Fe, New Mexico 87504

Printed in Mexico

Second edition. First printing February 1996

Library of Congress Cataloging-in-Publication Data
Lovett, Sarah, 1953–
Endangered species / text by Sarah Lovett ; [illustrations, Mary Sundstrom, Sally Blakemore]. — 2nd ed.
p. cm. — (Extremely weird)
Includes index.
Summary : Describes various endangered species, including the Vancouver Island marmot, orangutan, Houston toad, and babirusa.
ISBN 1-56261-280-8 (pbk.)
1. Endangered species—Juvenile literature. 2. Rare animals—Juvenile literature. [1. Rare animals.] I. Sundstrom, Mary, ill. II. Blakemore, Sally, ill. III. Title. IV. Series: Lovett, Sarah, 1953– Extremely weird.
QL83.L68 1995 95-50827
591.52'9—dc20 CIP
AC

Extremely Weird Logo Art: Peter Aschwanden
Illustrations: Mary Sundstrom, Sally Blakemore
Design: Sally Blakemore
Typography: Copygraphics, Inc., Santa Fe, New Mexico
Printer: R. R. Donnelley & Sons

Distributed to the book trade by
Publishers Group West
Emeryville, California

Cover photo: Marine iguana (*Amblyrhynchus cristatus*), courtesy Frans Lamting/Photo Researchers, Inc.

INTRODUCTION

"When we try to pick out anything by itself, we find it hitched to everything else in the universe."
—John Muir, Naturalist

There are more than five billion humans living on Earth. As our population grows, so do the problems we cause for the plants and animals sharing our planet. Because of us, species are disappearing at a scary rate. For the last 500 million years or so, scientists believe that species naturally became extinct at a rate of one or two each year. This year, scientists believe that at least 365 species will become extinct, maybe as many as 17,500. Extinction means there are no known living members of that species left anywhere in the world. In one month, between 30 and 1,400 species will disappear. In one day alone, we can say good-bye to at least one plant or animal species.

It's too late to save species that are already extinct. But what about those that are endangered? When the numbers of a particular species drop so low that it is threatened with extinction, it may be declared endangered. The U.S. government passed the Endangered Species Act in 1973. The purpose of that law is to protect endangered species from being killed or injured, having their habitats destroyed, or being illegally traded. "Endangered" means there's still time to help, but the law won't work without our support. The key to saving endangered species is us—making the planet a healthier place for all living things.

The most important thing we can do is control our own species' population. More and more people mean less and less room for other animals and plants. Conserving and recycling Earth's natural resources is another step, and so is encouraging others to do the same.

There's something else to think about. Scientists believe there could be as many as 80 million different species on Earth, so why should we care if many become extinct? After all, extinction is part of nature. The problem is that humans are hastening the process so that it is occurring at an *un*natural rate. Species are disappearing before we can even begin to understand precisely what their loss will mean to us.

All life on Earth is linked together. Every species needs other species to survive. And each plant and each animal plays a special part in keeping nature balanced. Since all things really are hitched together in the universe, even the tiniest termite is important!

To keep track of the millions of plant and animal species on Earth, scientists use a system called taxonomy. Taxonomy starts with the five main groups of all living things, the kingdoms, and then divides those into phylum, class, order, genus, and finally, species. Members of a *species*, the narrowest grouping, look similar, and they can reproduce with each other. In this book, the scientific name of each animal is listed next to the common name. The first word is the genus. The second word is the species.

You can help: Kids all around the world are doing their part to conserve our planet's resources. Kids bought (and saved) a rain forest in Costa Rica! Kids volunteer at the Clinch River Raptor Center in Tennessee to help wild birds recover from injuries and return to the wild! Kids helped protect the endangered prairie bush clover in Minnesota!

Hairy, Not Scary!

RED-KNEE TARANTULA (*Brachypelma smithi*)

Giant tarantulas, who cruise along on eight very hairy legs, are among the world's biggest spiders. Their bodies may grow to a length of more than 3 inches, and their legs may span a 9-inch area! These spiders look fierce and scary, and they're good hunters. They prey mostly on insects and help control buggy populations. Other spiders and birds hunt tarantulas. Among this spider's fiercest enemies are tarantula wasps. The wasps sting tarantulas and use the paralyzed spider bodies as food for wasp larvae.

MARY SUNDSTROM

Red-knee tarantulas from Mexico are ground-dwelling animals that live in burrows. They may dig their own hideaway or move into a burrow abandoned by rodents. They stay close to home and do their hunting within a few feet of their front door. When they're frightened, they can easily rush into the safety of the burrow.

Red-knee tarantulas are endangered because the land where they live is being developed by humans for logging, farming, and housing. Female tarantulas are not very portable, and a farmer's plow will destroy both the spider and her burrow. Fortunately, some farmers are leaving spider safety lanes, unplowed areas where spiders can move to safety. Being captured alive is another problem for tarantulas. Tarantulas taken from the wild are sometimes bought by people who want exotic pets.

SALLY BLAKEMORE

Just because spiders and other invertebrates aren't warm and furry, some people think they don't need our help. How many invertebrates are endangered? No one is really sure because it's very hard to count tiny creepy crawly critters. But scientists know that some species have become extinct before we even know they exist.

Green pitcher plant (*Sarracenia oreophila*), Courtesy Jeff Lepore/Photo Researchers, Inc.

Many plants, like the trumpet pitcher (*Sarracenia* spp.), are endangered species. Plants are the basic food source on Earth. These energy machines turn sunlight, water, and minerals from soil into food for animals like the maned wolf, the manatee, and you. Each plant species has other living things that totally depend on it for food. You might say we're all partners. When a plant becomes extinct, so can its partners.

© Michael Fogden/OSF

Fishy Fossil

GOMBESSA COELACANTH (*Latimeria chalumnae*)

How would you feel if you went fishing and pulled up a dinosaur in your net? Sound impossible? It is, since dinosaurs are extinct, but some animal species that lived 65 million years ago *are* still alive today. For instance, leatherback turtles and tuatara lizards are both very old species. So are some species of fish.

Not very long ago (in 1938), a captain of a South American fishing boat netted an extremely weird fish. The fish was a coelacanth (SEAL-ah-kanth), a species scientists had believed to be extinct for the last 80 million years or so. In fact, the real, live coelacanth was almost a fishy fossil. (It first appeared on Earth almost 400 million years ago.) Icthyologists (scientists who study fish) and others were very excited because this was a major scientific discovery.

Large, bony coelacanths belong to a group of fish named for the fleshy lobes at the base of their fins. Coelacanths grow to lengths of five feet, and they can swim backwards, upside down, and tails up! Because they have adapted to life in deep, deep water, coelacanths do not live long in captivity. Until scientists figure out a way to study them, they will remain mysterious fish.

Long before humans existed, extinctions were a fact of life. Dinosaurs ruled the Earth for more than 150 million years, but something happened 65 million years ago that wiped them out. Not only dinosaurs but winged pterosaurs, most large reptiles, many mammals, some birds and plants, and almost every kind of sea plankton disappeared. This was a mega-extinction! Was it caused by Earth's collision with an extraterrestrial force? No one knows for sure. Since humans and our ancestors have only existed for about 2 million years, we can only guess.

Loss of habitat (or living space), pollution, overhunting, and the introduction of new nonnative species (like sheep, rats, and cats) are four big threats to wild plants and animals.

Photo, facing page, courtesy Tom McHugh/Photo Researchers, Inc.

Take a Load Off a Toad

HOUSTON TOAD (*Bufo houstonensis*)

Freckled, moist, warty, eyes bulging, the Houston toad looks just like a. . .well, a toad! To human eyes, toads and other amphibians aren't all that beautiful. But they are extremely important: they prey on pesky insects, and they also help control mosquito populations. And while toads are eating small critters, larger predators, like snakes, bats, and rodents, are eating toads.

Houston toads depend on year-round and part-time wetlands to survive. They spend much of their time in sandy ground where they can burrow down. But to reproduce, Houston toads need water. Clusters of 500 to 6,000 eggs are deposited in flooded fields, rain pools, and ponds. Within days, tiny tadpoles emerge from the eggs. The tadpoles need at least two months to metamorphose (change) into froglets. If puddles or ponds dry up too soon, the tadpoles—left high and dry—will die.

In the 1950s, drought killed many Houston toads. Since that time, the cities of Houston and Austin, home to the Houston toad, have grown so large that wetlands have been drained and covered over with houses. New roads and sewage lines have changed natural drainage patterns and dried up ponds.

Fortunately, concerned humans have created a nature preserve for the Houston toad, and the Houston Zoo has helped increase toad numbers with a breeding program. Captive-bred toads are turned loose in the preserve where they can live without harm from humans.

This native amphibian of Texas has a mating call that some say sounds like a tinkling bell.

There's no denying the Houston toad is warty, but they're not the kind of warts that people get!

The International Union for Conservation of Nature has formed a special amphibian group as part of the Species Survival Commission to actively encourage amphibian conservation. Write: IUCN Species Survival Commission, C/O Chicago Zoological Society, Brookfield, IL 60503.

Photo, facing page, courtesy Tom McHugh/Photo Researchers, Inc.

Turtle Trouble

GALÁPAGOS TORTOISE (*Geochelone* spp.)

Tortoises wandered the Earth even before the age of the dinosaurs. They are the most ancient of reptiles, dating back 250 million years. They haven't changed a whole lot since then, either. If any tortoise looks as old and as wrinkled as time, it must be the giant of the Galápagos Islands off the coast of Ecuador. A full-grown Galápagos tortoise is 400 pounds of scaly, puckery skin, massive shell, and bowlegs. Tortoises are known for their amazing life span—sometimes as long as 150 years. But humans have made it difficult for tortoises to grow old.

In the 1800s, when the Galápagos Islands were discovered by European and American whaling vessels, sailors saw a great many tortoises. In fact, legends say a sailor could walk from island's end to end on the backs of the tortoises without touching the ground. The newly arrived humans killed tortoises for food. They also brought rats, cats, and dogs to the island, and those animals ate tortoise eggs and young turtles. Now, because their numbers have dwindled, Galápagos tortoises are an endangered species.

Turtles are the only reptiles with shells!

Another reptile, the American alligator, is a whole lot of help when it comes to keeping wetlands wet. These alligators create deep water holes and keep them free of weeds and muck. Even in the driest season, there's usually enough water left in these holes to keep turtles, fish, and snails alive. Some of these animals become food for mammals, birds, and alligators. But there are usually enough water-dependent animals left when the rains come to repopulate the wetland.

Some sea turtles, like the green sea turtle, *Chelonia mydas*, almost became extinct because humans valued its meat, eggs, and shell more than they valued the living creature. Although they are protected by law, green sea turtles will survive as a species only if humans stop killing them intentionally and accidentally in shrimp fishing nets.

Photo, facing page, courtesy Frans Lanting/Photo Researchers, Inc.

Rare Bird

HORNED GUAN (*Oreophasis derbianus*)

The horned guan wears a hat at all times. And an unusual hat, at that. The bright orangy red cap perched between the guan's eyes—and made of naked skin and bone—is in sharp contrast to the guan's glossy black body feathers.

Horned guan territory includes areas of southern Mexico all the way to Guatemala in South America. Although they do spend time on the ground, they are perfectly suited for life in trees. Horned guans build nests of twigs and leaves in the trees and bushes of mountain forests. On the move, they jump and tiptoe along the thinnest and highest branches and then take off on long gliding flights, only flapping their wings when absolutely necessary.

When they are surprised, horned guans have a loud, throaty cry almost like an explosion. Forest intruders are greeted with a chatter of yellow beaks that resembles the sound of a Spanish dancer's castanets.

These birds love bean sprouts, and they also eat flowers, berries, mangoes, guavas, and seeds. Most of the time, they search for food in trees or bushes, and they might even be seen hanging upside down (hats wiggling) as they eat.

Like many birds, horned guans are endangered because forests are being cleared to make room for people.

Pop it! Helium balloons are popular items at fairs and parties because they float up, up, and away. But those balloons are deadly to birds, sea turtles, and other marine life who mistake them for edible jellyfish. The balloons can stick in the animal's throat and suffocate it.

Conservation has a history. As far back as 242 B.C., the Indian emperor, Ashoka, created nature preserves for animals. Kublai Khan (1215?-1294) banned the hunting of birds at certain times of the year. And Incan kings in South America had a death penalty for any human who killed a seabird.

Photo, facing page, courtesy Tom McHugh/Photo Researchers, Inc.

Nature's Recyclers

CALIFORNIA CONDOR (*Gymnogyps californianus*)

One of the biggest flying birds in the world, adult California condors sometimes weigh as much as 20 pounds, and their wings may span 10 feet when spread. They can reach an air speed of 60 miles per hour and travel 140 miles per day foraging for food. Condors have no feathers from the neck up, where their wrinkled skin is gray, yellow, red, and orange. Their body is black except for a white underwing, and their scaly claws are as big as a man's hand. No doubt about it, they look extremely weird to humans.

In the wild, a typical condor day starts with a few hours of grooming and preening while perched on a tree branch or other roosting site. By midmorning, the condor sweeps over the countryside in search of food. Condors are vultures, their hooked beaks made to tear apart carcasses, and like other scavengers, they help clean up the countryside by eating the flesh of dead animals.

California condors used to nest in caves and rocky crevices in very lonely cliffs near the Pacific coast of California. Fossil records tell us California condors date back 100,000 years, and at one time they feasted on the flesh of saber-toothed tigers and mastodons. Although they once thrived throughout what is now the American West, modern life has become deadly for these birds.

It's hard to prove exactly what has made the California condor an endangered species. Scientists know that condors have been killed by hunters, and some have died from head-on collisions with power lines. Also, because condors feed on carrion, whatever killed their prey—often poisons and pesticides—can kill them, too. For all these reasons, there were only about 60 wild California condors left by the 1960s. By 1980, there were less than 30. Finally, the last birds were caught and moved to sanctuaries. Captive breeding programs have increased the numbers, and projects for reintroducing condors to the wild are under way. Scientists hope that these birds will once again thrive in the American West.

California condors, eagles, and falcons are all *raptors*, diurnal (active during the day) birds of prey that feed mostly on the flesh of other animals.

Animals are us! What we do to animals, we do to ourselves. And we have only one planet to share.

You can help: Write letters to the president of the United States, members of Congress, your state governor, and your city's mayor. Let them know you support the Endangered Species Act, and tell them what you think should be done to save endangered wildlife.

Photo, facing page, courtesy Tom McHugh/Photo Researchers, Inc.

Armor-dillo

GIANT ARMADILLO (*Priodontes giganteus*)

Armored in a double layer of horn and bone, the giant armadillo looks as weird as its relatives, the sloth and the anteater. How does the armadillo develop its armor? A baby armadillo is born with tough, leathery skin that hardens into horny plates or bands as it grows. This armored shell is very handy for hiding from other animals. And because the plates are surrounded by flexible skin, armadillos of some species can roll up into a ball when they are threatened. That's good protection for an armadillo's very vulnerable belly, which is covered with soft skin and hair instead of scales.

Adult giant armadillos may measure more than 4½ feet from head to tail's end and weigh as much as 130 pounds. They live in the forests of South America east of the Andes, from central Venezuela to northeastern Argentina.

The armadillo's tongue is shaped like a worm, and it has many small bumps covered with sticky saliva. These sticky bumps are great for catching ants, worms, spiders, and insects. But the giant armadillo's favorite food treat is a mouthful of termites. Because giant armadillos have claws and powerful limbs, they are very good diggers and scratchers. They can tear up termite hills in search of food and leave holes so big a human can fit inside.

Giant armadillos are endangered because unfortunately their skins have been valued by humans for handbags, luggage, and belts. Also, much of their homeland is being developed by humans for farming and housing.

Termites are some of nature's best recyclers. They break down dead wood so it can go back into the earth. Without termites, the world would be smothered by dead plants. Termites are worldly critters, but they prefer tropical climates. Termite colonies build mounds up to 30 feet high out of dirt and saliva. Inside, each individual—worker, soldier, or queen—has a job to do.

***Armadillo* is a Spanish word referring to the armorlike coat of this critter.**

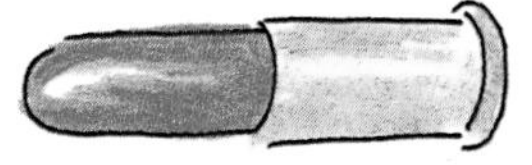

You can help: Don't buy cosmetics, jewelry, or leather goods that are made of wild animals! People who hunt wild animals commercially only do it because they can make money. If you're not sure what something is made of, or where it comes from, ask the salesperson.

Photo, facing page, courtesy Paul Crum/Photo Researchers, Inc.

Crying Wolf

Weird science! Scientists from the USSR decided to try to re-create the extinct mammoth by using a cell taken from a frozen bull in Siberia. They planned to implant the cell into an egg and uterus of a living female elephant. If it was done, the results have not been announced to the world.

MANED WOLF (*Chrysocyon brachyurus*)

From deep in the woodlands of central South America comes the cry, "Uaah uaah." Is it a bird? Is it a monkey? It might take you a long time to cry wolf—the maned wolf, that is.

The maned wolf, named for the thick dark mane along its back, is not closely related to other wolf species. Although it's about the same size as the true wolf (*Canis lupus*), its slender ears and sharp snout are more foxlike. The maned wolf travels alone except during mating season when pairs stay together.

Maned wolves are omnivorous, which means they eat plants *and* animals: fruits and nuts as well as rodents, birds, and even smaller animals. It's not unusual to see a maned wolf rooting for worms and snails among the leaves and grass of savannas and swamps. When they are hunting, maned wolves stop and start a lot. And they're always sniffing the air and wiggling their ears—the better to hear—as they search for prey.

When maned wolves play together, they charge full speed ahead and then leap into the air. This leaping ability comes in handy when they need to escape danger.

But humans are not easy to escape. Maned wolves are endangered by loss of habitat because people are clearing and burning the grasslands for farming. They are also hunted by people who fear the wolf will threaten domestic livestock.

Predators are animals that kill other animals for food. They are an important part of nature: their job is to keep their prey from having a population explosion.

Photo, facing page, courtesy Tom McHugh/Photo Researchers, Inc.

All a Goggle

SPECTACLED BEAR (*Tremarctos ornatus*)

Named for the white patches of fur that often surround its eyes, the adult spectacled bear might look as if it's wearing goggles. This large, black bear lives in high mountain forests of western Venezuela, Colombia, Ecuador, Peru, and western Bolivia. It is a shy, solitary animal who lives alone or in small family groups.

Spectacled bears enjoy a good climb. These agile animals build stick platforms high in the branches of trees. The platforms give them easy access to their favorite foods—leaves, shoots, and fruit. In some areas of their range, they munch on young palm plants and cactus. Every now and then, they may prey on other wild animals, like llamas, or cattle.

These bears are nocturnal (active at night). During the day, they bed down in caves, on tree trunks, or under large shady trees.

Fewer and fewer spectacled bears survive these days as humans move into their territory. They are killed for their meat and their skins, and they are hunted for "sport."

No opera star! The spectacled bear has an extremely weird, shrill voice.

Bears were worshiped by Stone Age cave-dwellers. Our ancestors kept bear skulls on poles and danced around them.

Even 2,000 years ago, humans were a problem for bears. Ancient European tribes hunted bears for skins, and Roman emperors staged bloody fights between bears, dogs, and gladiators.

You can help: Join National Wildlife Federation. This is the nation's largest conservation organization. For more than 50 years, NWF has worked to conserve wildlife and its habitat. NWF was instrumental in obtaining enactment of the Endangered Species Act in 1973 and has continued working to defend and strengthen that important environmental law. Write: NWF, 1400 16th Street, N.W., Washington, D.C. 20036.

Photo, facing page, courtesy Tom McHugh/Photo Researchers, Inc.

With a Twist

MARKHOR (*Capra falconeri*)

Markhors are wild goats with a twist. Their great horns grow in a pattern that seems a bit screwy —corkscrewy. Adult males use these horns to battle with each other to test who's strongest. When they are fighting, they turn their heads side to side so their horns clash like swords, and sometimes they rear up on their hind legs. Markhors also sport bushy beards, long hair, and thick manes. One of the largest species of goats, they can grow to a height of 100 centimeters (more than 3 feet).

Adapted for life at high altitudes where the air is thin and cold, these animals graze the rocky slopes of Asiatic mountains. They become active in the afternoon and evening when they search for grass, weeds, leaves, twigs, and shrubs.

Wild markhors breed from late summer to midwinter. Females usually give birth to one or two energetic kids. Mothers protect their young by fighting off intruders with their horns or by acting as a decoy for predators.

Markhors are threatened by loss of living space because of competition from humans and domestic livestock. They are also hunted for meat and their horns taken as trophies.

The markhor is an even-toed ungulate. That may sound like something squishy, but it really means a hoofed mammal with an even number of toes.

Great Grinders! A goat is an herbivore (plant eater) with no front teeth. It pulls its food with sturdy lips, tongue, tough upper gums, and small lower teeth. A goat's jaw moves front to back and side to side.

Some animals known only by their fossils were hunted to extinction by our early ancestors. The sivatherium was a close relative of the giraffe. And the 12-foot-tall marsupial named Palorchestes had a trunk, claws, and a long tail and looked extremely weird.

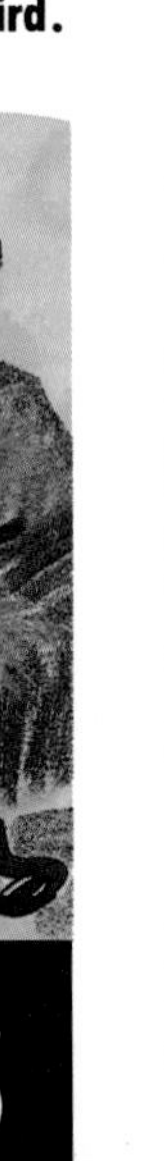
Photo, facing page, courtesy Tom McHugh/Photo Researchers, Inc.

Three Toes to Tapir

MALAYAN TAPIR (*Tapirus indicus*)

What's in a hoof? Odd-toed hoofed mammals come in a variety of sizes, shapes, and colors. What they have in common is the hard, bony hoof at the end of their legs and their toe count—an odd number. Rhinoceroses, horses, and tapirs are all odd-toed mammals. They look very different, but they are related.

The Malayan tapir sports a black coat with a broad white band in the middle—from just behind its front legs to the upper thighs of its back legs. This coat blends right in with the shadowy moonlit landscapes where it forages for food and also with the sunny riverbeds where it sleeps. (You've probably guessed that Malayan tapirs are active at night.) They live in lowland forests of Burma, Thailand, Sumatra, and the Malay Peninsula where they are able to find lots of water. They like to wallow in shallow rivers, and that may help them shake off mites, ticks, and other parasites.

Fossil remains prove that tapirs haven't changed much for many millions of years. All four tapir species still have a short trunk of a nose and four toes on their front feet and three toes on the back. They can weigh as much as 500 pounds and be up to 8 feet long.

Tapirs are endangered because they are hunted for food and because their habitat has been cleared by humans for agricultural purposes.

Check it out! The rain forests left on the planet contain at least 50% of the species on Earth. Hard to imagine that much life? Step out into your own backyard and pick one square foot of land. Now open your eyes. Are there beetles, ants, butterflies, spiders? In the rain forest, that same square foot would be home to at least ten times as many living things.

You can help: LightHawk is our nation's environmental air force. This nonprofit organization takes to the sky to target all sorts of environmental issues. For more information on action projects, write: LightHawk, P.O. Box 8163, Santa Fe, NM 87504-8163. You might even get to fly with LightHawk!

Hairy Horn

GREAT INDIAN ONE-HORNED RHINOCEROS (*Rhinoceros unicornis*)

Reaching a length of 13 feet, a shoulder height of 6 feet, and a weight of 2 tons, the great Indian one-horned rhinoceros doesn't look easy to push around. But this giant, now living only in a few areas of Nepal and eastern India, has been hunted almost to extinction mostly because of its one and only horn.

What's in a horn? Actually, a rhinoceros horn is made of hairlike growths. If you put it under a microscope, you wouldn't see individual hairs: rhino horns and hair are both made of keratin, a fibrous protein. For centuries, many Asian people have believed that rhino horn powder is strong medicine. And jewelry and daggers made of rhino horn are thought to bring human owners power. These traditions have taken a terrible toll on the rhinoceros. Poachers may earn more than $1,000 for each rhino horn, and in some places, that's more money than the average worker would make in two years. With profits like this, hunting continues even though it's against the law. So, one thing to do is to eliminate the demand for these "products."

Illegal hunting endangers *many* animals besides the rhinoceros. Great blue whales, cheetahs, African elephants, and mountain gorillas are all the victims of overhunting.

There are five species of rhinoceroses still living on earth. Two species have a single horn, like the Indian rhinoceros. The other three species have two horns growing in a row, one right after the other.

You won't mistake the great Indian rhinoceros for its relatives in Africa because its skin, which has lots of loose folds, resembles a giant suit of armor. African rhinos, in contrast, are fairly fold-free.

Photo, facing page, courtesy S. Nagendra/Photo Researchers, Inc.

African elephants are illegally hunted for their ivory tusks. A tusk is a great tooth that keeps on growing and growing. The average elephant will produce about half a ton of ivory in a lifetime.

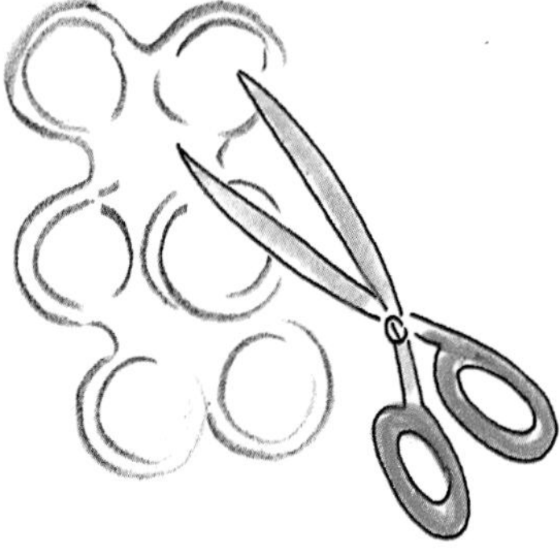

Scoop the loop! Plastic loops that ring six-pack cans get tossed out with the garbage and often end up floating in our planet's oceans. When loops get caught around the necks of baby birds, seals, otters, and other animals, they are deadly. If you find loop litter, make sure the plastic gets cut up into tiny pieces so it can't harm another animal.

WEST INDIAN MANATEE (*Trichechus manatus*)

Chubby, neckless, wrinkly, and tuskless, the gentle mammals known as manatees spend much of their time munching on sea vegetables in shallow ocean waters. In fact, a grown-up manatee can devour 100 pounds of plants each day. Although they may weigh as much as 3,500 pounds and grow longer than 12 feet, these aquatic mammals are very graceful swimmers. Propelled by spoon-shaped tails and flippered forelimbs, manatees slowly graze coastal waters, sometimes cruising 150 miles in one summer.

Manatees seem to occupy most of their day eating and playing—they trade gentle kisses, nibbles, and caresses—in warm waters. And sometimes, they will bob up to a boat to be petted. In the United States, where they are protected by the Endangered Species Act, their only enemies are human vandals and power boats. Because they live along the shores and rivers of Florida and Caribbean islands, manatees are in constant danger of injury or death from speeding motorboats. Most living manatees encountered by scientists have many scars from boat collisions. Humans can help manatees by treating them with respect and slowing down their boats, or, better yet, by avoiding waters in which manatees live.

Manatees belong to the class Sirenia. Sailors on long, long voyages have been known to mistake swimming manatees for mermaids and singing sirens.

Manatees are relatives of elephants, and they have been swimming in Earth's oceans for more than 45 million years.

Photo, facing page, courtesy Douglas Faulkner/Photo Researchers, Inc.

DOUC LANGUR (*Pygathrix nemaeus*)

Douc means monkey in Vietnamese, and the douc (pronounced "duke") langur is one of the world's most beautiful monkeys. This primate's almond eyes and smooth cheekbones give it the look of a wise and gentle scholar. Its glossy fur and white wispy beard add a touch of mystery. The douc langur lives in the tropical forests of Laos and Vietnam where it spends daylight hours searching for leaves and fruit to eat.

The douc langur is in danger of becoming extinct. During the Vietnam War, chemical weapons and bombs proved deadly to these primates. Much of their habitat was destroyed, and soldiers living in the jungles killed them for food. War is a human tragedy. It is also an ecological disaster with horrible consequences for wildlife.

Homo sapiens **(like us) have been around for more than 600,000 years. Neanderthal man came a bit later, but he's been extinct for about 40,000 years. No one knows for sure, but scientists believe that Neanderthal man may be extinct because our human ancestors exterminated him.**

It costs money to create nature preserves and conservation programs. Many nations (and people) are too poor to do it on their own and need help from richer nations like the United States. If we help poorer nations meet their people's needs for adequate food, housing, and employment, the push to destroy wildlife habitat just to survive will be reduced.

You can help: Don't buy wild animals! Every time someone pays for a pet that was taken from the wild, he or she encourages trappers to catch more. Ask your local pet store owner to sell only animals that have been raised in captivity.

GLOSSARIZED INDEX

This glossarized index will help you find specific information about endangered animal species. It will also help you understand the meaning of some of the words used in this book.

African elephants, 26
African rhinoceros, 26
American alligator, 10
amphibians—animals (like frogs and salamanders) that have a backbone and moist skin, that spend part of their life cycle in water, and that depend on their outside environment for body heat, 8
bears, Romans and, 20
bears, Stone Age cave dwellers and, 20
blue whales, 26
Brachypelma smithi—red-knee tarantula, 4
Bufo houstonensis—Houston toad, 8
California condor (*Gymnogyps californianus*), 14
Canis lupus—true wolf, 18
Capra falconeri (markhor)—an endangered species of wild goat, 22
captive breeding programs—programs to breed captive animals, especially endangered species, 14
carnivore—flesh-eater, 18
cheetahs, 26
Chelonia mydas—green sea turtle, 10
Chrysocyon brachyurus—maned wolf, 18
class—third-largest taxonomic grouping of living things, 3
condor, fossil records, 14
dinosaur extinctions, 6
douc langur (*Pygathrix nemaeus*)—endangered primate, 30
economics and conservation, 30
endangered birds, 12, 14
Endangered Species Act—law passed by the U.S. government in 1973 in an effort to protect endangered species from being killed or injured, from having their habitats destroyed, or from being illegally traded, 3, 14, 20
endangered species—a species is said to be endangered when its numbers drop so low that its survival is threatened, 3
extinction—when there are no known living members of a species (like the dodo bird), 3
Galápagos Islands—islands off the coast of Ecuador known for unique and diverse wildlife, 10
Galápagos tortoise (*Geochelone* spp.), 10
genus—second narrowest taxonomic grouping of living things, 3
***Geochelone* spp.**—Galápagos tortoise, 10
giant armadillo (*Priodontes giganteus*), 16
Gombessa coelacanth (*Latimeria chalumnae*), 6
great Indian one-horned rhinocerous (*Rhinoceros unicornis*), 26
green sea turtle (*Chelonia mydas*), 10
Gymnogyps californianus—California condor, 14
habitat, human, 18
habitat, loss of, 6
helium balloons, as a threat to sea animals, 12
herbivore—plant-eater, 22
Homo sapiens—human species, 30
horned guan (*Oreophasis derbianus*), 12
Houston toad (*Bufo houstonensis*), 8
Icthyologists—scientists who study fish, 6
Incan kings and conservation, 12
Indian emperor Ashoka and conservation, 12
International Union for Conservation of Nature—worldwide conservation group, 8
invertebrates—animals that do not have backbones (i.e., insects, snails, worms), 4
kingdoms—the five main taxonomic groups of all living things, 3
Kublai Khan, and conservation, 12
Latimeria chalumnae—Gombessa coelacanth, 6
leatherback turtles, 6
LightHawk—nonprofit environmental air force especially concerned with forest conservation, 24
Malayan tapir (*Tapirus indicus*), 24
maned wolf (*Chrysocyon brachyurus*), 18
markhor (*Capra falconeri*)—endangered species of wild goat, 22
metamorphosis—when a body form changes between egg, larval, and adult stages, 8
mountain gorillas, 26
National Wildlife Federation—the largest conservation organization in the United States, 20
Neanderthal man, extinction of, 30
nonnative species, introduction of, 6
odd-toed ungulate—hoofed mammal that has an odd number of toes, 24, 26
omnivore—animal that eats plants and animals, 18
order—fourth-largest taxonomic grouping of all living things, 3
Oreophasis derbianus—horned guan, 12
overhunting, as a threat to wildlife, 6
Palorchestes—extinct marsupial, 22
phylum—second-largest taxonomic grouping of all living things, 3
plastic loops, a danger to sea animals, 28
poachers—humans who illegally kill or capture endangered animals, 26
pollution, as threat to wildlife, 6
predator—animal that kills other animals for food, 18
primates—group of mammals that includes monkeys, apes, humans, 30
Priodontes giganteus—giant armadillo, 16
Pterosaurs, 6
Pygathrix nemaeus—douc langur, 30
rain forest conservation, 24
red-knee tarantula (*Brachypelma smithi*), 4
reptiles, endangered, 10
rhinoceros horn, value to humans, 26
Rhinoceros unicornis—great Indian one-horned rhinoceros, 26
Sirenia—scientific class of manatees, 28
sivatherium—extinct relative of the giraffe, 22
species—narrowest taxonomic grouping of living things, 3
spectacled bear (*Tremarctos ornatus*), 20
Tapirus indicus—Malayan tapir, 24
taxonomy—scientific system of classification for all living things, 3
termites, natural recyclers, 16
tortoise, endangered, 10
Tremarctos ornatus—spectacled bear, 20
Trichechus manatus—West Indian manatee, 28
true wolf (*Canis lupus*), 18
trumpet pitcher plant (*Sarracenia* spp.), 4
tuatara lizards, 6
war, as an ecological disaster, 30
West Indian manatee (*Trichechus manatus*), 28